the Country Friends®
Collection

POTATOES

Mary Elizabeth ... mashes potatoes with her Grandma's old red-handled masher.

Kate ... likes mashed potatoes best when cold.

Holly ... thinks her trusty mixer makes the best mashed potatoes.

Let's go **Potato Shopping**

... there are over ★ 5000 ★ varieties to choose from!

Buy: Firm, Smooth, Clean Potatoes

... well-shaped fellas!

YES

Avoid: Bruised, Soft, Cut, Sprouted Potatoes

NO!

> To be good is noble. To tell people how to be good is even nobler and much less trouble.
> — MARK TWAIN —

2

Generally speaking,
here are the different kinds of
POTATOES
you're likely to find at the market:

RUSSET ... GOOD FOR BAKING & FRYING!

LONG Whites ... BOILING POTATOES!

Round Whites ... BOIL 'em, MASH 'em, FRY 'em!

Round Reds ... GREAT BOILERS!

So many Potatoes, So little time!

There are SO many different varieties of potatoes — and we LOVE their colorful names:

YuKon GOLD   COWHORN

candystripe   Snow flake

PURPLE Marker   cherry JuBiLee

STORE Your SPuDS

Keep your potatoes in a cool, dark spot, unwashed and unwrapped. Don't store them with apples or onions (they'll spoil each other) and don't refrigerate or their starches will turn to sugar.

HEY! TURN OFF THAT LIGHT!

Farm ★ Style Potato Pancakes

a recipe from Wendy Paffenroth ★ Pine Island, NY

5 POTATOES, PEELED & GRATED
1·½ T. ALL-PURPOSE FLOUR
½ t. SALT
⅛ t. PEPPER
2 T. onion, GRATED

2 EGGS, BEATEN
⅛ t. PAPRIKA
⅛ t. DRIED PARSLEY
2 T. OIL

— ✳ —

Combine all ingredients except oil; drop by spoonfuls into hot oil. Brown on both sides; drain. Serve hot. Makes 5 servings.

Grow Your Own!

Potatoes grow best in well-aerated soil with lots of moisture. Plant in a different spot each year, but never plant where tomatoes have grown ∽ they are subject to the same diseases!

I Consider it the best part of an education to have been born and brought up in the Country.
— A.B. Alcott —

Garden Glories!
Stuffed Potatoes

a delicious recipe from Kristine Marumoto ★ Sandy, UT

4 russet potatoes, baked
2 T. butter
1 onion, finely chopped
10-oz. pkg. frozen broccoli,
    thawed & drained

1 c. shredded Cheddar cheese
½ c. ranch salad dressing
1 T. oil
2 t. dried parsley
salt & pepper to taste

★

Carefully slice off about ½-inch of the top of each potato; scoop out the potato, keeping skins intact. Mash the removed potatoes ~ set aside. Sauté onion in butter until tender; remove from heat and add broccoli, salad dressing & cheese. Combine with mashed potatoes ~ mix well. Brush potato skins with oil; spoon mixture into shells, dividing evenly. Place on baking sheet and bake at 425 degrees for 15 minutes. Sprinkle with parsley, salt & pepper.
Makes 4 servings.

TATER PATCH

COUNTRY ★ FRIENDS ★

6

Herbed New Potatoes

a delightful recipe from
Linda Shively ★
Hopkinsville, KY

2 lbs. new potatoes
2 T. water
¼ c. butter, melted
2 T. fresh parsley, minced and divided
1 t. fresh basil, minced

*

Prick each potato with a fork; place in a 13" x 9" baking dish. Add water ~ cover with plastic wrap and microwave on high for 11 minutes, or 'til tender. Drain water; set aside. Combine butter, one tablespoonful of parsley & basil together in a small mixing bowl; pour over potatoes, tossing lightly to coat. Sprinkle with remaining parsley. Makes 8 to 10 servings.

Farming looks mighty easy when your plow is a pencil, and you're a thousand miles from a corn field.
— DWIGHT EISENHOWER —

COUNTRY FRIENDS'
New Potatoes

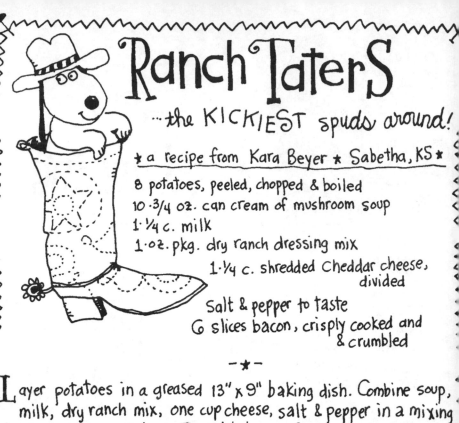

Ranch Taters

...the KICKIEST spuds around!

★ a recipe from Kara Beyer ★ Sabetha, KS ★

8 potatoes, peeled, chopped & boiled
10·3/4 oz. can cream of mushroom soup
1·1/4 c. milk
1·oz. pkg. dry ranch dressing mix
1·1/4 c. shredded Cheddar cheese, divided

Salt & pepper to taste
6 slices bacon, crisply cooked and & crumbled

— ★ —

Layer potatoes in a greased 13" x 9" baking dish. Combine soup, milk, dry ranch mix, one cup cheese, salt & pepper in a mixing bowl; pour over potatoes. Top with bacon & remaining cheese; bake, uncovered, at 350 degrees for 25 to 30 minutes or until potatoes are tender. Makes 10 servings.

⌐KNOW YOUR⌐
POTATO HISTORY

CHAPTER ONE:

YUM!

Francisco Pizarro happened upon the potato as he was exploring around Quito, Ecuador in the 1500's... he described it as a "TASTY, MEALY TRUFFLE." He carried it back to Spain when he went home.

German Potato Salad

...an old favorite!

a recipe from
Kathryn Benkow
★ East Aurora, NY

12 potatoes, peeled, boiled & chopped
1 onion, diced
1 T. salt
½ t. pepper
¼ c. fresh chives, chopped
½ c. oil
2/3 c. cider vinegar

*

Combine potatoes with onion, salt, pepper & chives in a large serving bowl; drizzle oil over mixture. Pour vinegar over potatoes; toss thoroughly. Serves 12.

A BIG STONEWARE BOWL FULL OF POTATOES MAKES A WONDERFUL RUSTIC CENTERPIECE FOR A SOUP DINNER ⌣ enjoy their earthy texture!

WOW!

According to the Guiness Book of World Records, Willie Newgent of Armagh, England holds the record for potato chip consumption: He ate 30 bags (without a drink) in 24 minutes, 33.6 seconds.

The Quechua Indians of Peru have over 1000 words for potato!

JoAnn's GREAT GARLIC MASHED POTATOES

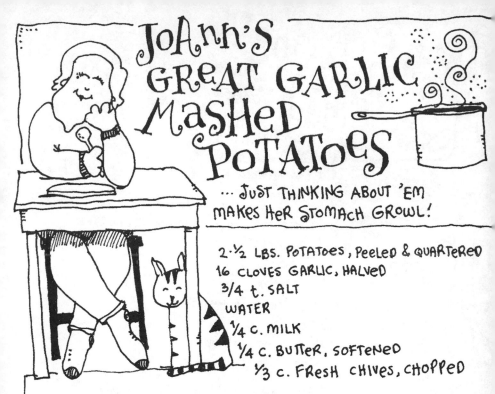

... JUST THINKING ABOUT 'EM MAKES HER STOMACH GROWL!

2·½ LBS. POTATOES, PEELED & QUARTERED
16 CLOVES GARLIC, HALVED
3/4 t. SALT
WATER
¼ C. MILK
¼ C. BUTTER, SOFTENED
⅓ C. FRESH CHIVES, CHOPPED

Place potatoes, garlic & salt* in a saucepan, cover with water and bring to a boil. Boil gently for 15 to 20 minutes or until tender; drain. Mash potatoes & garlic until smooth; add milk & butter. Beat mixture until fluffy; stir in chives. Makes 8 to 10 servings.

POTATO HISTORY

To: LIZ♥
from: Walt

CHAPTER TWO :

Back when taters were an unknown veggie, Sir Walter Raleigh made a gift of spuds to Queen Elizabeth 1. Her cooks, being unfamiliar with potatoes, threw out the tuber parts and boiled the stems & leaves for a big palace party... BIG mistake! Guests were poisoned by the cuisine and potatoes were banned from the Queen's court for years.

HEARTY HOME·FRIES

a recipe from
JEAN PFANKUCH
★ CHIPPEWA FALLS, WI

1·½ LBS. RED POTATOES, PEELED
& QUARTERED

1 T. OIL
2 SHALLOTS, SLICED
1 t. PAPRIKA
½ t. DRIED ROSEMARY
½ t. DRY MUSTARD
¼ t. SALT
⅛ t. PEPPER

★

Sauté potatoes in oil on
medium heat for 4 minutes;
turn and cook until almost
tender — about 3 minutes.
Add remaining ingredients;
simmer until tender. Serves 6.

KATE'S BAD·BUT· BODACIOUS

◉ BAKED POTATO TOPPERS:

· BUTTER · LOTTA   So
· CHEESE SALT   WHAT.
· BACON   I LIKE
· MORE BUTTER   BAD
· CHOCOLATE CHIPS   STUFF.

★ F.Y.I. ★

POTATOES ARE LOW
IN CALORIES — AN
AVERAGE LARGE
POTATO ONLY HAS ABOUT
140 CALORIES IN IT...

WHEN YOU START ADDING
ALL THE GOOD·TASTING·BUT·
NOT·GOOD·FOR·YOU STUFF,
THE CALORIE COUNT JUMPS

↑UP!↑

TRY SOME
OF THESE TASTY
TOPPERS ON YOUR
NEXT BAKED POTATO...
THEY'RE

★GOOD★ FOR YOU.

Mint	Onions	Lemon Juice
Garlic	Cayenne pepper	
Dill		Green peppers
Chives	Salsa	
Caraway seeds	Parsley	Peas
Basil	Olive oil	Broccoli Florets
Thyme		Tomatoes
Rosemary	Mustard	

The great source of pleasure
is VARIETY.
—Samuel Johnson—

11

·POTATO·PUFF· CASSEROLE

Hey, mom — What's for dinner?

FROM TINA ALBRECHT ★ MESA, AZ

1 lb. ground beef, browned
16-oz. can French cut green
    beans, drained
3-oz. can French fried
    onion rings
16-oz. pkg. frozen potato puffs
10-3/4-oz. can cream of chicken
    soup

3/4 c. milk
1 t. salt
1/4 t. pepper
1/8 t. paprika

★

Layer beef in a 2-quart baking dish; top with layers beginning with green beans, then onion rings and finally, potato puffs. In a separate mixing bowl, combine soup, milk, salt and pepper; pour over layers. Sprinkle with paprika; microwave on high 20 minutes, turning twice. Serves 6.

QUICK and GOOD!

You'll love

Turkey Tater Nuggets

a recipe from TRACEY MONNETTE ★ ROSEVILLE, MI

.. a great way to put Thanksgiving leftovers to use!

1 c. cooked turkey, cubed
2 c. mashed sweet potatoes
2 eggs, beaten
4 T. milk

¼ t. nutmeg
1·½ c. plain bread crumbs,
divided
2 T. oil

★

Combine turkey, potatoes, eggs, milk, nutmeg and 3/4 cup bread crumbs ⌄ mix well. Form mix into nuggets ; coat each with remaining bread crumbs. Lay nuggets on wax paper ; set aside for 10 minutes. Heat oil in medium skillet ; cook nuggets for 4 to 5 minutes, flip and cook another 3 to 4 minutes. Drain on paper towels ; serve warm. Serves 4.

Be eating ONE potato, peeling a SECOND, have a THIRD in your fist, and your eye on a FOURTH. ⌄ IRISH SAYING

Dear Santa,
All I want for Christmas
is your recipe for

Holiday Potatoes

a recipe from TONYA PRICE ★
RUSSELLVILLE, KY

8 YUKON GOLD POTATOES,
  PEELED, CUBED & BOILED
½ c. BUTTER
8-oz. CARTON SOUR CREAM
½ c. ONION, FINELY CHOPPED
¼ c. GREEN BELL PEPPER,
  FINELY CHOPPED
¼ c. DICED PIMENTO
1 EGG, BEATEN
16-oz. PKG. SHREDDED
  CHEDDAR CHEESE

Drain & mash potatoes; add butter, sour cream, onions, green pepper & pimento. Mix until butter is melted; add egg and blend well. Spread mixture in a 13"x9" greased baking dish; bake at 350 degrees for 20 minutes. Sprinkle cheese over the top; bake for additional 10 minutes. Serves 6 to 8.

The red pimento & green peppers make a festive dish!

It's smart to do your holiday hinting early.

— ARNOLD GLASOW —

Hmmm.... Gee, Holly ~ I sure do LOVE your mashed potatoes.... Mary Elizabeth, just where do you think I could find a potato bowl just like yours? .... Uh, Vickie & Jo Ann....

14

May Peace and Plenty
be the first
To lift the latch
on your door,
and
Happiness
be guided to
your house
by the
candle
of
Christmas.

– old blessing –

The sprouts and green spots on a potato contain SOLANINE, which is potentially toxic so carve those out of your taters!

FAMILY·FOLK·Potatoes

a recipe from Laurin Gibson
♥ Wrentham, MA

...great for a family dinner.

6 c. red potatoes, peeled & chopped

1 onion, chopped

8·oz. carton sour cream

8·oz. pkg. shredded Monterey Jack cheese

8·oz. shredded Cheddar cheese

¼ c. butter, melted

½ t. salt

½ t. pepper

1·½ c. breadcrumbs

Boil potatoes & onion together until tender; drain. Mix in sour cream, cheeses, butter, salt & pepper; spoon into a greased 2·quart baking dish. Sprinkle breadcrumbs on top; bake at 350 degrees for 30 minutes.
Serves 8.

Hash Brown Quiche

a winter's day recipe from
JEAN GALLANT ★ NEW BEDFORD, MA

3 c. frozen shredded hash browns,
          thawed
⅓ c. butter, melted
1 c. cooked ham, diced
1 c. shredded Cheddar cheese
¼ c. green pepper, diced
4 eggs
½ c. milk
½ t. salt
¼ t. pepper

Press hash browns onto the bottom and up the sides of an ungreased 9-inch pie plate; drizzle with butter. Bake at 425 degrees for 25 minutes. Combine ham, cheese & green pepper; spread onto crust. Beat eggs, milk, salt & pepper in a mixing bowl; pour into crust. Bake at 350 degrees for 25 to 30 minutes or until a knife inserted near the center comes out clean. Let stand 10 minutes before cutting. Makes 8 servings.

Heaven give you many, many merry days!

~SHAKESPEARE~

16

Victorian Ladies in England kept a hot potato inside their muffs to keep their hands warm!

Skaters' Tater Soup

a warming recipe from Melissa Dunne ✱ New Lenox, IL

4 T. dried parsley
1 T. margarine
6 c. chicken broth
4·½ c. red potatoes, cubed

¾ c. carrots, sliced
1 zucchini, cubed
1 c. cooked chicken, cubed

✱

Combine all ingredients in a large saucepan; simmer for 20 to 30 minutes or until vegetables are tender. Serve warm. Makes 6 servings.

WHAT I SAY is

THAT IF A MAN REALLY LIKES

POTAToES,

He MUST Be A PRETTY DECENT SORT OF FeLLoW. ~ a.a. miLne

SPUD:

A Version of THE GAME OF DODGE BALL ~ EVERY THROWN BALL THAT MISSES A RUNNER IS CALLED A SPUD!

1 POTATO, **2** POTATO, **3** POTATO, **4**,
5 POTATO, **6** POTATO, **7** POTATO,
MORE.
~ OLD·TIME RHYME

★ LADIES, CLIMB INTO YOUR SNEAKERS FOR THE

Potato Relays!

A Player must pick up a potato in a spoon, carry it across the room and deposit it in a pan. SHe then runs back, and hands the empty spoon to a teammate, who must run to the pan, pick up the potato in the spoon and bring it back … so it goes until the whole team has run. And what does the winning team receive? You decide, but we suggest an extra·helping of homemade mashed potatoes would be a *grand prize!*

★ **FYI** : the Bengali name for potato is BILATI LOO.

Country Morning Breakfast Potatoes

a recipe from Christine Richardson
* Wadsworth, IL

4 potatoes, baked
1 onion, chopped
1 green pepper, chopped
4 ·oz. can sliced
    mushrooms
1 tomato, chopped
1 c. shredded Cheddar
    Cheese
1 c. Monterey Jack
    Cheese

Chop cooled potatoes; set aside. Sauté onion, pepper & mushrooms in a large skillet. Add potatoes & tomato.

Pour into a greased 2-quart baking dish; top with cheeses and bake at 350 degrees until melted. Serves 4.

Have an early morning come·as·you·are party!

BREATHE IN... OUT...
THERE'S NOTHING WRONG
WITH YOU THAT A
LITTLE BIT
OF

CRAZY
Potato
Candy
WON'T CURE!

A RECIPE FROM
LESLIE STIMEL
★ GOOSEBERRY PATCH

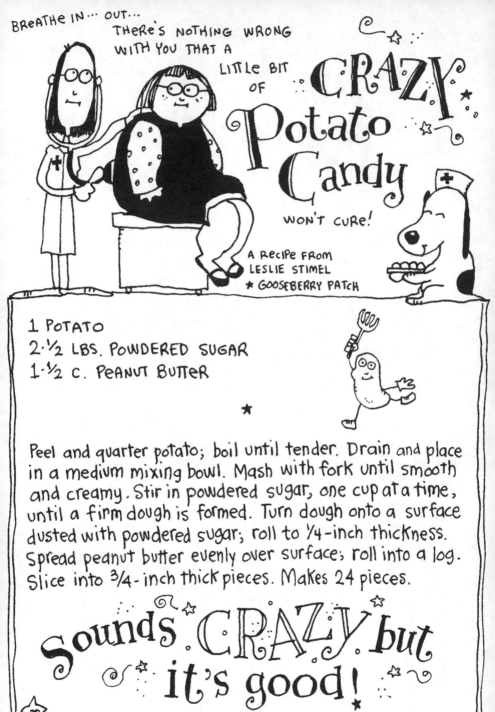

1 POTATO
2·½ LBS. POWDERED SUGAR
1·½ C. PEANUT BUTTER

★

Peel and quarter potato; boil until tender. Drain and place
in a medium mixing bowl. Mash with fork until smooth
and creamy. Stir in powdered sugar, one cup at a time,
until a firm dough is formed. Turn dough onto a surface
dusted with powdered sugar; roll to ¼-inch thickness.
Spread peanut butter evenly over surface; roll into a log.
Slice into ¾-inch thick pieces. Makes 24 pieces.

Sounds CRAZY but it's good!

Life's more amusing than we thought. -Andrew Lang

Heavenly!
POTATO DONUTS

a YUMMY recipe from ROXANNE BIXBY
★ W. Franklin, NH ★

2 c. mashed potatoes, cooled
2 T. butter
1 c. sugar
2 eggs
2 t. baking powder
1 t. nutmeg
1 t. baking soda
½ t. salt
½ c. buttermilk
4 c. all-purpose flour
oil for deep-frying

★

Beat mashed potatoes and butter until creamy. Add sugar, eggs, baking powder, nutmeg, baking soda and salt ~ blend well after each addition. Pour in milk and flour alternately into potato mixture. Roll dough out on lightly floured surface to ¼-inch thickness; cut out with donut cutter. Add enough oil to a deep-fryer to equal 4 inches. Heat oil to 375 degrees and add 3 or 4 donuts at a time. Turn when golden ~ drain on paper towels. Makes about 30 donuts.

Eat Your Taters.

Do You Know HOW GOOD THEY ARE FOR YOU?

RICH in VITAMIN C.

a good source of enzymes and minerals and other good stuff.

Eat UP.

COUCH POTATO CHIPS

a recipe from
★ CYNTHIA SMITH PLEASANTON, KS. ★

2 SWEET POTATOES
1·½ T. CHILI POWDER
1 t. SUGAR

½ t. CUMIN
1 t. SALT

★

Slice potatoes lengthwise into very thin slices and pat dry with a paper towel; spread onto a baking sheet. Mix together remaining ingredients; sprinkle half over slices. Bake at 325 degrees for 15 minutes, then turn slices over, sprinkle with remaining spices and bake an additional 15 minutes. Place on a wire rack to cool and dry. Serves 2.

AHem.
Technically Speaking...

The sweet potato isn't really a potato. It grows under the ground like a potato, but is actually a member of the morning glory family.

The West Indian name for sweet potato is "BATATA"... the English word "POTATO" is probably a derivation of that... a case of mistaken identity!

Praline Sweet Potato Casserole

...Why, I do declare! It's mighty tasty, Miz Holly!

a fine recipe from VICKIE BOROUGHF ★ Johnstown, CO

3 c. sweet potatoes, peeled, cooked & mashed

2 eggs

1 c. sugar

½ c. sweetened condensed milk

¼ c. butter

1 t. vanilla extract

Combine ingredients; pour into 10" x 8" baking dish. Sprinkle with topping. Bake at 350 degrees for 35 minutes. Makes 6 servings.

Topping:

5 T. butter, melted
1 c. brown sugar, packed
⅓ c. all-purpose flour
1 c. chopped pecans

Mix ingredients together until it resembles coarse crumbs.

Folklore: A flower on the potato vine means generosity for the planter.

Sweetie Pie
SWEET POTATO CASSEROLE

a recipe from Michelle Hedrick ★ Belleville, IL

40-oz. can cut sweet potatoes, drained

8-oz. can crushed pineapple, drained

½ c. maple syrup

½ c. pecan halves

¼ c. sliced dried apricots

¼ c. brown sugar, packed

1 T. butter, melted

1 t. cinnamon

1 t. pumpkin pie spice

¼ t. salt

*

Place the sweet potatoes in an ungreased 1.½ quart baking dish; set aside. Combine the remaining ingredients; pour over potatoes. Bake uncovered at 350 degrees for 45 minutes or until heated through. Makes 8 to 10 servings.

Let the sky RAIN potatoes.

— SHAKESPEARE —
"THE MERRY WIVES OF WINDSOR"

DID YOU KNOW THERE IS A POTATO MUSEUM IN GREAT FALLS, VIRGINIA?

Home Sweet Homestyle Sweet Potato Biscuits

BAKE A BASKET-FULL, GET OUT THE BUTTER & EAT!

a melt·in·your·mouth recipe from KATHY GRASHOFF ★ FORT WAYNE, IN

2 c. all-purpose flour
2·½ t. baking powder
½ t. salt
¼ c. butter, softened

¼ c. shortening
1 c. sweet potatoes, peeled,
  cubed & boiled
6 T. buttermilk

★

Combine flour, baking powder and salt in a large mixing bowl; cut in butter and shortening until well blended. Mash potatoes and add to flour mixture. Stir in enough buttermilk to form a soft dough; lightly knead 20 times. Roll out dough on a lightly floured surface to ½·inch thickness; cut into biscuits. Bake at 450 degrees on an ungreased baking sheet for 12 to 15 minutes or until a light golden brown. Makes 2 dozen.

MOST -LIKELY -UNTRUE -BUT- OH- SO- INTERESTING -&- AMAZING

Potato Lore:

★ Hang a piece of dried potato 'round your neck in a bag to prevent rheumatism.
★ Rub half a 'tater on a wart... bury the potato and by the time it rots away, the wart will be gone.
★ Carry a spud in your pocket to cure a toothache.

25

amazing! POTATO SLANG

"POTATO TRAP" (the mouth)

Impress your family & friends with your wide knowledge!

"SPUD": THOUGHT TO HAVE ORIGINATED IN SCOTLAND OR ENGLAND IN CONNECTION WITH THE SPADE ~ A DIGGING FORK USED TO DIG 'EM UP!

"CROAKERS" "LUMPERS" "MICKEYS"

... all Irish nicknames for the beloved potato.

Going on a long Sea Voyage?

Take along a sack o'taters ~ they store better than citrus and are high in Vitamin C ~ good for treating scurvy!

USS TATO

JUST GIVE ME MY POTATO, ANY KIND OF POTATO, AND I'M HAPPY.
—Dolly Parton—

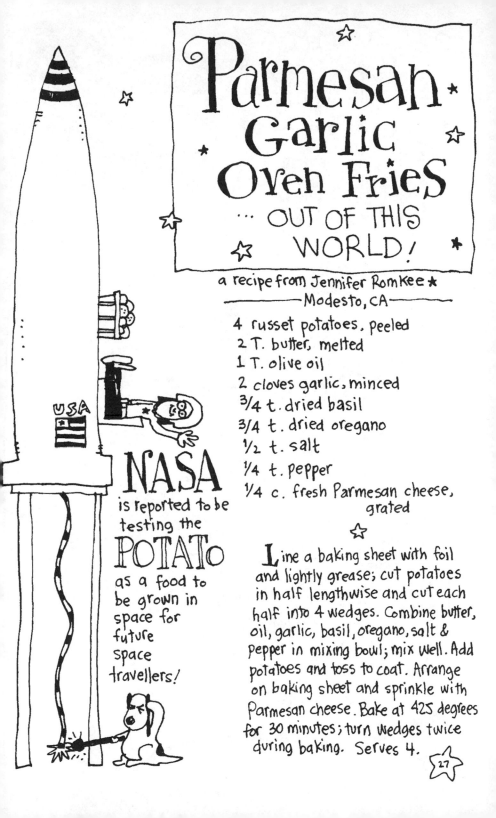

Parmesan Garlic Oven Fries

... OUT OF THIS WORLD!

a recipe from Jennifer Romkee
— Modesto, CA —

NASA is reported to be testing the **POTATO** as a food to be grown in space for future space travellers!

4 russet potatoes, peeled
2 T. butter, melted
1 T. olive oil
2 cloves garlic, minced
3/4 t. dried basil
3/4 t. dried oregano
1/2 t. salt
1/4 t. pepper
1/4 c. fresh Parmesan cheese, grated

Line a baking sheet with foil and lightly grease; cut potatoes in half lengthwise and cut each half into 4 wedges. Combine butter, oil, garlic, basil, oregano, salt & pepper in mixing bowl; mix well. Add potatoes and toss to coat. Arrange on baking sheet and sprinkle with Parmesan cheese. Bake at 425 degrees for 30 minutes; turn wedges twice during baking. Serves 4.

27

YUMMY Summer Favorites

Summery Potato ★ Salad ★

a recipe from Dawn Mays ★ Stuarts Draft, WV

2 LBS. POTATOES, BAKED
3/4 c. SOUR CREAM
3/4 c. MAYONNAISE
8 SLICES BACON, CRISPLY
COOKED & CRUMBLED
1/2 c. RED ONION, CHOPPED

1/2 C. CELERY, CHOPPED
1/2 t. SALT
1/4 t. PEPPER
GARNISH: GREEN
ONIONS, SLICED &
SHREDDED CHEDDAR
CHEESE

Coarsely chop cooled potatoes into 1/2-inch cubes; set aside. Combine remaining ingredients in a separate mixing bowl ⌐ toss with potatoes, cover & refrigerate overnight. Garnish with onions & cheese if desired. Serves 12.

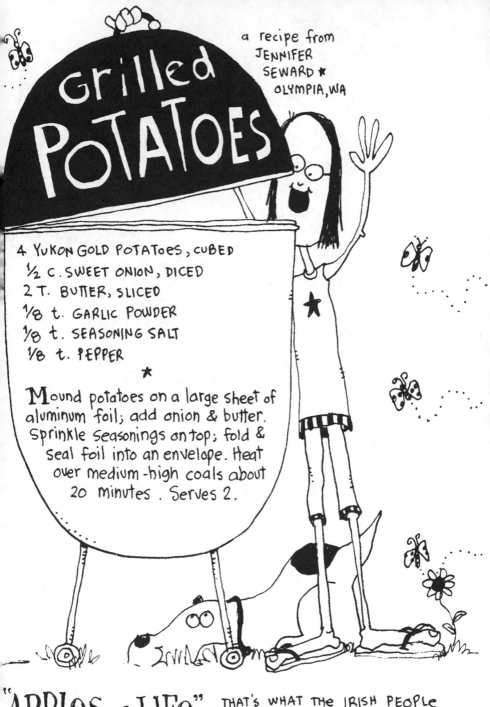

Grilled POTATOES

a recipe from JENNIFER SEWARD ★ OLYMPIA, WA

4 YUKON GOLD POTATOES, CUBED
½ C. SWEET ONION, DICED
2 T. BUTTER, SLICED
⅛ t. GARLIC POWDER
⅛ t. SEASONING SALT
⅛ t. PEPPER

*

Mound potatoes on a large sheet of aluminum foil; add onion & butter. Sprinkle seasonings on top; fold & seal foil into an envelope. Heat over medium-high coals about 20 minutes. Serves 2.

"APPLES of LIFE": THAT'S WHAT THE IRISH PEOPLE CALLED THE POTATO IN THE EARLY 19TH CENTURY. BY THAT TIME, A TYPICAL IRISH FAMILY OF G PEOPLE MIGHT HAVE CONSUMED UP TO 250 POUNDS OF POTATOES A WEEK ～ POTATOES WERE A MIGHTY STAPLE IN THE IRISH DIET!

SERVE UP A POTATO PICNIC!

Warm Mustard Potato Salad

a recipe from Vickie ★ Gooseberry Patch

2 lbs. red potatoes, boiled
1 c. mayonnaise
¼ c. Dijon mustard
⅔ c. red onion, chopped
2 green onions, sliced
2 cloves garlic, minced
3 T. fresh dill, chopped
½ t. salt
½ t. pepper
¼ t. lime juice

*

Drain potatoes and cool slightly. Combine remaining ingredients; set aside. Cut potatoes into chunks; place in a serving dish. Add mustard mixture; gently toss to coat. Makes 8 to 10 servings.

That one who does not get FUN and Enjoyment out of every day in which he lives, needs to reorganize his life. And the sooner the better....
— GEORGE MATTHEW ADAMS —

Picnic Potato Rolls

··· DELICIOUS WITH
A CHUNK OF HAM
FOR LITTLE PICNIC
SANDWICHES!

a recipe from Gay Snyder
★ Deerfield, OH ★

1 pkg. active dry yeast
1½ c. warm water
2/3 c. shortening
2/3 c. sugar
2 t. salt
2 eggs
1 c. warm mashed
     potatoes
5½ c. all-purpose flour,
     divided

*

Sprinkle yeast over warm
water; set aside until foamy,
about 5 minutes. Add
shortening, sugar, salt, eggs,
mashed potatoes & 2 cups
flour; mix 'til smooth. Work
in the remaining flour; place
dough in a greased bowl. Cover;
let rise overnight in refrigerator.
Divide & shape into 24 balls;
place on a greased baking
sheet. Let double in bulk; bake
at 350 degrees for 10 to 20
minutes or until golden brown.
Makes 24 rolls.

Recipe Index